Reptiles

Reptiles

HERON BOOKS

Published by
Heron Books, Inc.
20950 SW Rock Creek Road
Sheridan, OR 97378

heronbooks.com

Special thanks to all the teachers and students who
provided feedback instrumental to this edition.

ISBN: 978-0-89-739284-6

Printed in the USA

31 October 2022

LEARNING
at the
SPEED
of You

At Heron Books, we think learning should be engaging and fun. It should be hands-on and allow students to move at their own pace.

To facilitate this we have created a learning guide that will help any student progress through this book, chapter by chapter, with confidence and interest.

Get learning guides at
heronbooks.com/learningguides.

For teacher resources,
such as a final exam, email
teacherresources@heronbooks.com.

We would love to hear from you!
Email us at *feedback@heronbooks.com.*

IN THIS BOOK

Chapter 1

How Are Reptiles Alike?

How Are Reptiles Alike?

A group of animals that is alike in some important ways is called a **class**.

One class of animals is reptiles. This class includes snakes, lizards, turtles and crocodiles. Reptiles are one of the oldest kinds of animals on Earth. They have been around for 300 million years!

Long before there were any birds or mammals, there were reptiles. In fact, many scientists who study animals believe that birds and mammals developed from reptiles long ago. The dinosaurs were closely related to reptiles. The dinosaurs are all gone but many reptiles similar to the reptiles that lived with the dinosaurs are still here.

Reptiles are alike in certain ways.

REPTILES HAVE DRY SCALY BODIES

Scales are thin, hard, rounded little plates that reptiles have on their skin instead of hair or fur. The scales help protect the reptile's body. Most reptiles have overlapping scales like fish, but some have scales that do not overlap.

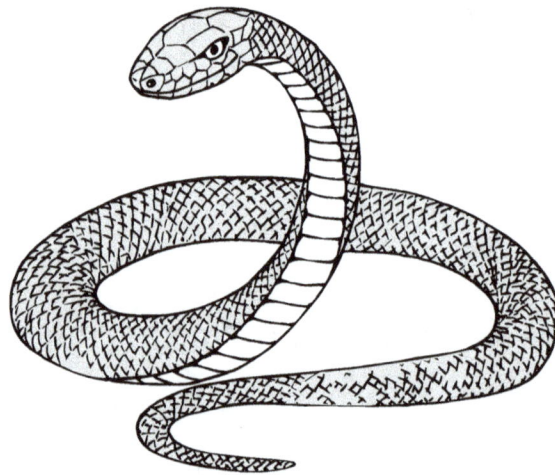

REPTILES HATCH FROM EGGS

Most reptiles hatch on land in a nest made by the mother. Although some reptiles spend most of their time in water, they lay their eggs on land. The shells are generally leathery and tough, not hard and easy to break like bird eggs.

Quite a few snakes and some lizards do not lay their eggs. Instead the eggs hatch inside the mother, and the young are born from the mother alive (already hatched). Some water snakes have young that are born this way right in the water.

REPTILES ARE COLD-BLOODED

Cold-blooded doesn't mean that their blood is really cold. It just means that their bodies change temperature as the temperature of the air around them changes.

On cold days, reptiles move slowly because their bodies are cold.

On warm days, reptiles' bodies are warmer and they can move quickly.

Since reptiles depend on the sun and the air around them to keep them warm, most reptiles live in the warmer areas of the world. No reptiles live in the very cold places of the world. If an alligator, for example, gets in water that is too cold, its muscles stop working and it will sink to the bottom and drown.

HOW ARE REPTILES ALIKE?

They have hard scales on their bodies instead of hair or fur.

They hatch from eggs.

They are cold-blooded.

LET'S DO THIS!
How Reptiles Are Alike

To do this activity you will need

- access to the internet or books or magazines of reptiles (if desired as an alternate for some internet images)
- drawing materials

Steps

DRY SCALY BODIES

1. Look at pictures of reptile scales.

2. Notice what is similar and different about them.

3. Look for scales that overlap and scales that don't.

HATCH FROM EGGS

4. Look at pictures of reptile eggs and reptiles hatching.

5. See if you can tell that the eggs are leathery, and different from bird eggs.

COLD-BLOODED

6. Decide if the place you live is mostly warm or cold.

7. Do you think many reptiles live there?

8. If so, where might they live, and when do you think you might be able to find them?

9. Write or tell another person your answers, and why you think so.

PUT IT TOGETHER

10. Draw a picture of a reptile, including something to show the temperature of the air and the temperature of the reptile. Show the scales and the eggs. Label the drawing with three ways reptiles are alike.

11. Show your drawing to another person, and explain the three ways reptiles are alike.

Chapter 2

The Life of a Reptile

The Life of a Reptile

GETTING STARTED

When reptiles are grown, they **mate**. This means a male and female get together so they can make babies.

After they have mated the female lays her eggs. She lays them in a place where the sun will keep them warm. Sometimes she covers them with sand or with grass and leaves to help keep them warm at night. Snakes sometimes lay their eggs under rocks.

After that, most female reptiles go off and leave the eggs alone. Many of the eggs may be eaten by other animals before they hatch, especially when they are left unguarded. But usually some survive, and soon there will be more baby reptiles.

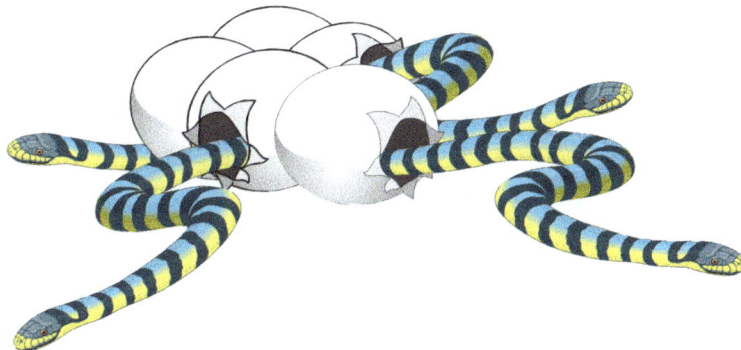

GROWING UP

Baby reptiles can eat and take care of themselves as soon as they are born. They eat the same things and live the same way as adult reptiles. But since baby reptiles are small, many of them get eaten by birds or other animals before they grow up.

Many reptiles eat insects. Some snakes eat small animals such as birds, mice and frogs. Crocodiles eat fish and even larger animals such as deer and pigs! Some lizards may eat plants as well as insects and other animals. Turtles eat plants and berries, fish and other water animals, and some insects.

Since reptiles are cold-blooded, they depend on the sun and air to keep warm. After a cold night, reptiles will often crawl slowly into a sunny place to warm up.

When they are warm, they can move quickly to catch their food. Lizards are most active during the day.

If they stay in the sun too long, their bodies get too hot. Then they have to crawl into the shade to cool off.

Most reptiles can go several days without food or water. When they do eat or drink, they eat or drink enough to last them a long time.

Adult reptiles may live a very long time. Lizards and snakes often live more than 20 years, alligators more than 60 years, and land turtles have been known to live over 150 years, giving them the world record for long life!

During their lifetimes these reptiles may mate many times, so even if most of their eggs and babies get eaten, there are still a lot of baby reptiles to grow up and become adults.

Chapter 3

So Many Reptiles!

So Many Reptiles!

All of the kinds of reptiles alive today can be put into four groups. These four groups are turtles, lizards, snakes and crocodiles. (The crocodile group includes alligators.) Of course, there are many different kinds of turtles, lizards, snakes and crocodiles.

TURTLES

The kind of reptile most easily found in most parts of the United States are turtles. The most common turtles live in small, weedy ponds. On a summer day they can often be seen sitting on a log or a rock, warming themselves in the sunshine.

There are many different types of turtles. Most turtles are green, brown or gray and some have very colorful markings on their shells, bellies, feet and head.

All turtles have hard shells on their backs.

shell

The shells are made of bone covered with very hard scales. The shells are protection for the turtles. Turtles cannot run away fast like other animals. When an enemy is near, instead of running away the turtle pulls its head, legs and tail under the shell. The hard shell keeps the enemy from hurting the turtle.

One kind of turtle, called the box turtle, even has a hinged shell. This means the shell can bend on the hinges. So, after pulling its head and legs inside the shell, it can close up the openings.

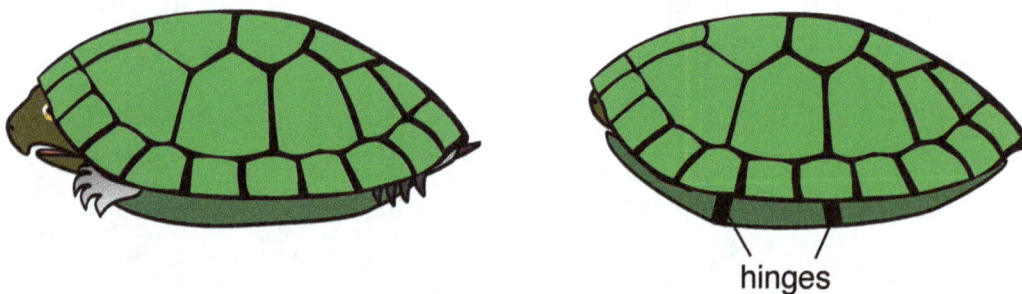

hinges

Some kinds of turtles live on land. These are sometimes called tortoises. Tortoises eat plants, insects and small animals. They can get very big. The largest tortoise in the world can grow more than 4 feet long and weigh 900 pounds!

Other kinds of turtles live in rivers, lakes and oceans. Another name for some of these turtles is terrapin. Some of these turtles (or terrapins) eat fish, and others eat pond weeds and other plants.

The most common fresh water turtle in most of the United States is the painted turtle. It gets its name from the red and yellow lines that mark its shell and even its neck and legs. They can grow to be up to 9 inches long, but most that you see will be smaller.

One kind of turtle in the United States is the snapping turtle. This turtle grows up to 17 inches long and can weigh 50 pounds. A snapping turtle can stretch its neck out almost as long as the rest of its body, and is likely to snap at you with its strong jaws if you disturb it when it is on land. Snapping turtles live in quiet, muddy-bottom water in most of the United States except the western part.

Turtles that live in the oceans are called sea turtles. The largest turtle of all is a sea turtle that can grow to be 8 feet long and weigh 1200 pounds! It is called the leatherback turtle because its shell is covered with skin instead of scales. Like other sea turtles, the leatherback's feet are shaped like flippers for swimming.

Other kinds of turtles are only a few inches long. They are sometimes kept as pets in a terrarium. A **terrarium** is something like an aquarium for fish, but it has both water and dry places such as sand and rocks in it, so the turtle can get in the water and also has a dry place to crawl out on.

Turtles can live longer than any other animal. Some tortoises live to be 150 years old. This is older than the oldest person!

SNAKES

All snakes are reptiles. There are many kinds of snakes with different colors and sizes. Some kinds, such as the common garter snake, are usually only about two feet long and are completely harmless.

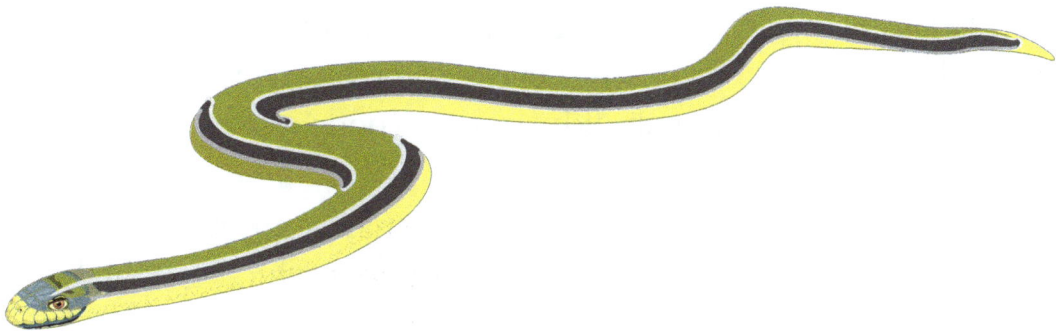

Other kinds, like the python in India, grow to be thirty feet long and can be very dangerous.

All snakes have smooth, dry, scaly bodies and no legs. They have one row of extra wide scales down the length of the belly that they use to help them crawl. Snakes have no eyelids, so they can never close their eyes. They have forked tongues that they use to help them smell.

Snakes shed the outer layer of their skin several times a year. They just crawl right out of it, leaving it all in one piece, including the clear scales that cover over their eyes. Sometime you might be lucky enough to find a snakeskin in the woods.

Some snakes have poisonous bites. Most snakes are not poisonous and are safe to handle. You just have to know which is which.

The cobra is a poisonous snake found in parts of Asia. It is unusual because of the way it can spread its neck to look like a hood.

Poisonous snakes can kill with their bites. You can tell most of the poisonous snakes in the United States (rattlesnakes, for example) by their broad triangular head. These snakes have long teeth called **fangs** that they use to inject poison when they bite.

The "rattle" of a rattlesnake is at the end of its tail. Each time it sheds its skin it gets one new rattle part. It rattles its tail when it is warning you to stay away.

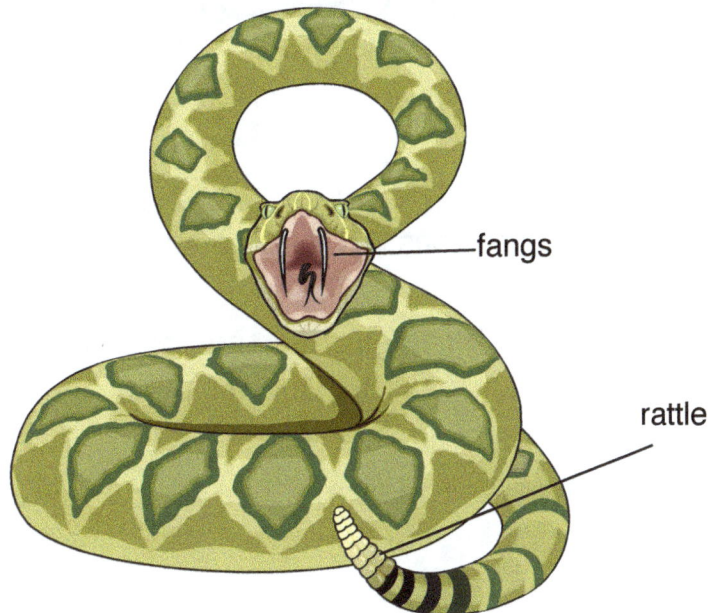

fangs

rattle

Some other snakes, like the python, kill by coiling around and squeezing their victim until it is crushed or can't breathe. These are called constrictors (*con-* means "together" and *-strict* comes from a word meaning "draw tight or squeeze").

Big constrictors can squeeze a human to death. These big constrictors mostly live in the tropics. No constrictors dangerous to humans live in the United States.

Snakes eat insects and small animals, and sometimes eggs of other animals. All snakes swallow their food whole. They do not chew it. If the food is too big, the snake's jaws come apart and its mouth stretches until everything goes down. A small snake can swallow an egg bigger than its head without breaking the egg. A big snake can swallow a whole pig! After it is swallowed, the meal makes a big lump in the middle of the snake.

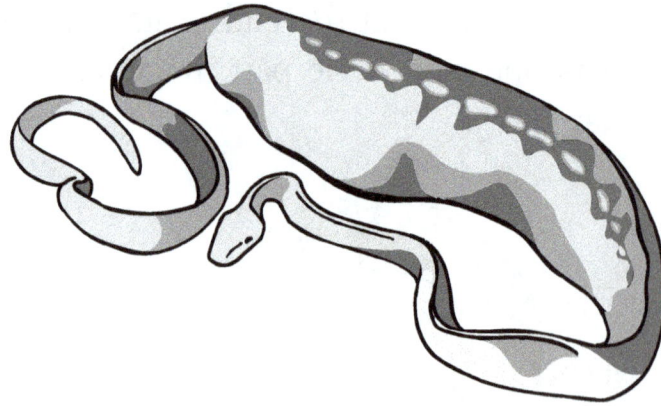

This python has swallowed a wild pig.

When it has swallowed a big meal like this, a snake may lie still for days or even weeks while it digests the food.

Some snakes live in the ground, some live in trees, and others on rocks.

Others live near water and can swim.

Most snakes are helpful to people because they eat animals and insects that are bothersome to humans.

LIZARDS

Lizards are reptiles that walk or run with their bellies very close to the ground. Most lizards have four legs, long thin bodies and claws on their toes.

Some kinds are only two inches long when full grown. The biggest lizard in the world is the Komodo dragon of Indonesia. It can grow to be ten feet long!

Some lizards are brightly colored but most are a brown or gray color. Some live in deserts and some live in wet jungles. Others live in forests and fields. None live where it is very cold.

Lizards eat mostly small animals like insects, spiders and earthworms. Some bigger kinds of lizards also eat snails, small mammals and other lizards.

Some lizards, like the horned toad (which is not really a toad at all), have fat bodies, and horns and spines on their skins to protect them from enemies.

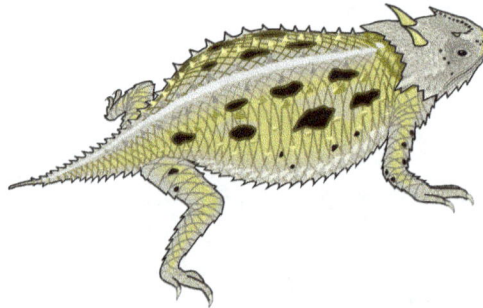

Other lizards, usually called skinks, are very slender and look almost like a snake with legs.

There are even some lizards that have no legs at all. They started out with legs long, long ago, but over the many, many years, they got smaller and smaller until they were gone. It is not easy to tell they aren't snakes, but they have eyelids and the same size scales on the belly as on the back. Legless lizards are actually fairly common in many parts of the United States, but usually people who see them think they are snakes.

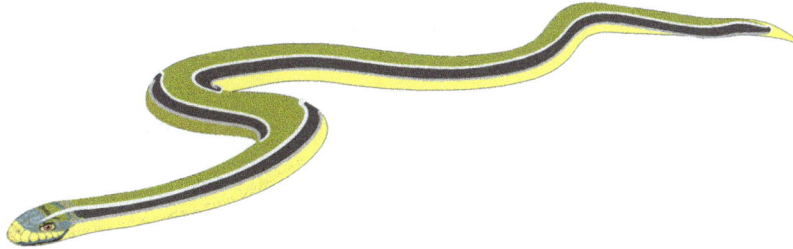

Very few lizards have poisonous bites, but one that does is the gila (HEE-la) monster of the southwestern deserts of the United States. It is not much of a monster, being only two feet long.

Some lizard's tails will easily break off from the body. This way the lizard can escape if caught by the tail. The tail will wiggle while the lizard runs away, and fool the enemy into thinking it caught a whole lizard. The lizard will then grow a new tail.

Some lizards appear to have an extra eye! This third eye on top of the head is not a real eye, but it is covered by a transparent scale and is connected to a part of the lizard's brain. Nobody knows if this extra eye can see anything.

Chameleons (ka-ME-lee-ons) are a very odd type of lizard that lives in trees, mostly in Africa and southern Asia.

Their bodies are much fatter than most lizards and their backs arch higher. Some have horns on their head. Their legs and feet are made for holding small tree branches, with half the toes turned backward. They are the only lizards that have curly tails. A chameleon can use its tail like an extra foot and hold onto a branch by wrapping its tail around it.

Chameleons do not move quickly like most lizards. They walk very slowly along branches and stems of plants, looking for insects.

Another odd thing about chameleons is their eyes. The eyes are covered with scaly eyelids, except for the small hole they see through. And each eye can move separately, so a chameleon may turn one scaly eyeball to look at you while it is swiveling the other eye around searching for insects.

When a chameleon spots an insect, it shoots out its tongue and catches the insect on the tongue's sticky tip. The tongue of a chameleon is as long as its whole body, and shoots out so quickly it can snag an insect in mid-flight.

As if these things were not strange enough, chameleons also change the color of their skin! They are usually a dull brownish-green. But when they are angry or afraid, they turn bright green. When they are cold or hungry, they turn yellow-gray. When the males mate, they turn bright red. Chameleons may also turn almost black or speckled or other colors depending on how hot or cold it is.

All of these color changes are automatic. The chameleon cannot "decide" to change its color. And unlike what people once thought, they can only make small color changes to match their surroundings in order to hide.

Most chameleons are one foot long or less, but some kinds grow to be two feet long.

Another kind of lizard, the little anole (uh-NO-lee), changes color from green to brown somewhat like a chameleon. The anole is common in the southeastern United States and some tropical islands. It is often called a chameleon and is even sold as an "American chameleon" in some pet stores in this country. But the anole looks like an ordinary lizard, not like a true chameleon at all.

The anole has a bright red throat fan that it displays when it is angry.

CROCODILES AND ALLIGATORS

Crocodiles are the largest of all living reptiles. They often grow to be 15 feet long and weigh over 1,000 pounds! Crocodiles are a dull green, gray or brown.

Crocodiles live in warm jungles and swamps in the tropics. They always live near water. Young crocodiles eat fish and small animals. Large crocodiles eat bigger animals such as deer or wild hogs. They kill these animals by clamping them in their strong jaws and pulling them under water until they drown.

Alligators are closely related to crocodiles. Alligators are found in warm, swampy places in the southeastern United States. They eat small animals and fish. The easiest way to tell an alligator from a crocodile is that the alligator's snout is blunt, and the crocodile's is longer and more pointed.

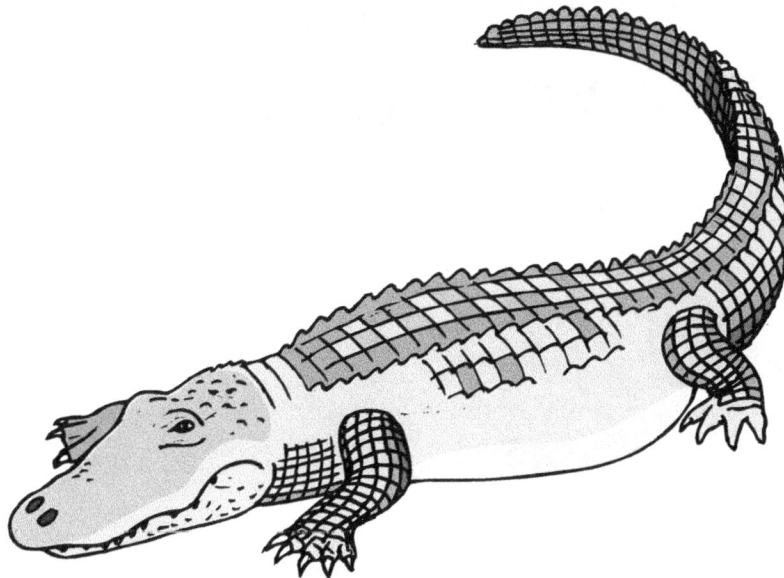

A crocodile or alligator's jaws are very strong for closing its mouth and holding its victim, but quite weak for opening it. People who catch alligators try to hold the jaws shut and tie them shut to make them less dangerous.

Alligators are one kind of reptile that have a big voice. They can make a very loud roaring, booming sound.

WERE DINOSAURS REPTILES?

Dinosaurs are a kind of animal that lived very long ago. We can tell from the bones of the dinosaurs that we find today what they probably looked like.

Some were very large, others were small. Some ate plants and others ate animals. All of them died out long ago.

We know from studying dinosaur bones that they were *related* to reptiles, but we don't know for sure if they were true reptiles. Some people think they were, and they were all cold-blooded. Others believe that at least some of them were probably warm-blooded, and more like featherless birds. With only old bones to tell by, people may argue about this for a long time.

In any case, the only reptiles still alive today are turtles, lizards, snakes and crocodiles.

LET'S DO THIS!
Find Out More

For this activity you will need

- access to internet
- drawing materials

Steps

1. Choose at least three kinds of reptiles you would like to learn about. You can find out more about one of the reptiles discussed in this book, or choose a different kind of reptile. To get an idea of which retiles to choose, you can search for "different kinds of reptiles." Some that you might find are mud turtles, spotted turtles, map turtles, loggerhead turtles, iguanas, glass lizards, blind snakes, water snakes, hognose snakes, racer snakes, coral snakes (very poisonous!) and whip snakes.

2. Write down the reptiles you chose.

3. Have an adult help you find a short online video or article for children about the reptiles you chose. Find out about your reptiles, including their names, where they live, what they eat, and some things you thought were interesting about them. Take notes so you can use them when you answer questions later.

4. Draw a picture of each of your reptiles. Try to make your pictures show what makes each of these reptiles special.

5. Show your drawings to another person, and answer any questions.

Chapter 4

Living with Reptiles

Chapter 4

Living with Reptiles

Reptiles have had a place in the world ever since the time of the dinosaurs. Because they are cold-blooded, they don't use up much energy keeping their bodies warm like warm-blooded animals. For this reason, they can live without food for a long time.

So, many reptiles can survive during difficult times when birds and mammals cannot find enough to eat, such as during a long, dry season. Then when conditions change and many quick-growing insects appear, the reptiles have survived and are there to eat the insects.

Reptiles are an important part of a food chain. A **food chain** is nature's way of making sure all the creatures of the world get fed. Every living thing is a part of a food chain. One kind of animal might eat plants, then that animal becomes food for another kind of animal, and that animal becomes food for another kind of animal, and so on like a chain. Reptiles eat lots of insects and other small animals, then later they become food themselves for bigger animals. Owls and hawks, for example, often eat lizards and snakes. Foxes and wolves and lions also sometimes catch and eat these reptiles.

Reptiles eat many insects which otherwise would bother people and other animals. Some reptiles also eat mice and gophers and other small animals that otherwise would eat farmers' crops. This makes these reptiles helpful to have around.

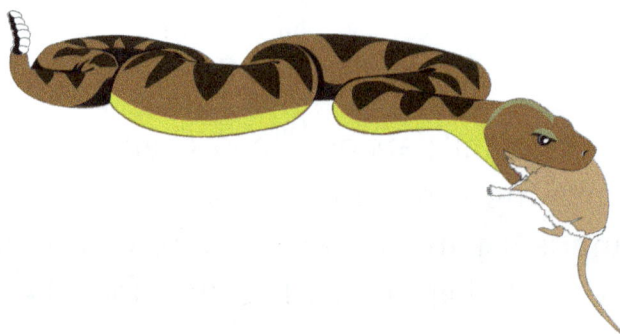

Sometimes reptiles even provide food for people. People in some parts of the world eat turtles and turtle eggs, and some people eat lizards and snakes. There are people who would tell you that turtle soup is the best-tasting soup there is.

Certain kinds of reptiles can be dangerous to people, such as poisonous snakes. It is a good idea to know which snakes are poisonous, and leave these snakes alone! It is also wise to learn first aid for snake bite before walking into country where there may be some poisonous snakes.

Crocodiles and alligators may also be very dangerous. Sometimes these large reptiles attack people who get too close, especially if it is a mother guarding a nest where her eggs are hatching.

People sometimes affect reptiles in a bad way, too. Some people are afraid of snakes and think all snakes are bad. They kill snakes whenever they can, even the ones that are really good.

Reptiles have their place in the world, and the person who knows about them can live with them successfully, avoiding the dangerous ones and encouraging the helpful ones.

LET'S DO THIS!
More Activities with Reptiles

TAKE CARE OF A PET REPTILE

For this activity you will need

- access to a pet reptile
- drawing materials

Steps

1. Get permission to take care of the pet reptile every day for a few days.

2. Find out how often the reptile need to be fed and what it eats, and anything else that needs to be done to take care of it.

3. Find out what kind of reptile it is, and where it originally comes from.

4. Find out what the natural food is for your reptile.

5. Try to find out something you didn't already know about the reptile.

6. Look closely at your reptile. See what it likes to do during the day. Look at its head, feet and tail. Notice its scales, and, if possible, pick it up and look at its belly. Feel the scales, and notice if it feels cold or warm. If it is a turtle, look closely at its shell. Tap the shell gently to see if it pulls its legs and head under the shell.

7. Draw a picture of it.

8. Write or tell another person what you found out, and show your picture.

STUDY WILD REPTILES OUTSIDE

For this activity you will need

- access to a park or nature area where there are wild reptiles
- drawing materials

Steps

1. Find out what kind of reptiles live in your area and where they might be found.

2. Go to a park or nature area where you might be able to find them.

3. If it is a warm day, go to some open ground or a field and look for lizards on rocks and snakes in grass. If you see one, watch for as long as you can and see what it is doing.

4. If there is a pond, go there and look for turtles around the pond's shore. If you see any, watch them for as long as you can and see what they are doing.

5. Learn the names of the reptiles you found, and what they eat.

6. Draw pictures of them, and label the pictures.

7. Write or tell another person what you learned, and show your drawing.

STUDY REPTILES IN A PET STORE

For this activity you will need

- access to a pet store that has reptiles
- drawing materials

Steps

1. Go to a pet store where they have reptiles. Tell the person in charge of the store why you are there and ask permission to study the reptiles.

2. Look at all the reptiles, and pick one or more that you like best.

3. Find out what their names are, what they eat, and how to take care of them.

4. Draw a picture of your reptiles, and write the name of it on the picture.

5. Write or tell another person about what you learned, and show your pictures.

STUDY REPTILES AT A ZOO

For this activity you will need

- access to a zoo
- drawing materials

Steps

1. Go to a zoo and look at all the reptiles.

2. Pick at least three kinds of reptiles that are your favorites.

3. Draw a picture of each one, and put the name of the reptile on each picture.

4. Find out where they come from, what they eat and how they live, and write that down too.

5. Write or tell another person about what you what you learned, and show your pictures.

STUDY REPTILES AT A MUSEUM

For this activity you will need

- access to a science museum that has a reptile display
- drawing materials

Steps

1. Go to a science museum and look at all the displays about reptiles.

2. Pick your favorite display and draw a picture of it.

3. Learn all you can from the display about the one you picked. If this was not a big display with more than one type of reptile in it, find another one you like and draw a picture of it too.

4. Keep doing this until you have learned all about at least three types of reptiles.

5. Write or tell another person what you learned, and show your drawings.

WATCH A VIDEO ABOUT REPTILES

For this activity you will need

- access to internet
- globe or map
- drawing materials

Steps

1. Have an adult help you find a short online video for children about a kind of reptile that you want to learn more about. Watch the video, and notice things you have already learned about reptiles, like what makes them reptiles, the different parts of their lives, and so on.

2. Look at a globe or map to find the place where the reptile in the video lives.

3. Decide what parts of the video you liked best, and draw pictures to show what happened in that part.

4. Write or tell another person what you have learned about reptiles that you noticed in the video, and show your drawing.

DO YOUR OWN SPECIAL REPTILES PROJECT

Steps

1. Think of a project about reptiles that you can do that isn't on this list. For example, maybe you know someone who studies reptiles and takes pictures of them, and you can learn about that.

2. Tell another person what you want to do, and how you will do it.

3. Do your project.

4. Write or tell another person everything you did, and what you learned.